AF269993

MY VOICE

A GUIDE TO MASTERING LIFE, TRUTH, AND PURPOSE

RALPH CLOTAIRE JEAN

SUPREME LEGACY PRESS

My Voice: A Guide to Mastering Life, Truth, and Purpose
First Edition

Copyright © 2026 by Ralph Clotaire Jean
Published by Supreme Legacy Press
Tallahassee, Florida

ISBN 979-8-9948806-2-3 (hardcover)
Library of Congress Control Number: 2026902224

Cover and interior design by Ralph Clotaire Jean

Printed in the United States of America

This book is a work of nonfiction reflecting personal insight, lived experience, and individual perspective. It is intended solely for educational, motivational, and personal development purposes. Nothing in this book should be interpreted as professional medical, psychological, legal, financial, or therapeutic advice. Readers should consult qualified professionals regarding any health concerns, legal matters, financial decisions, or personal challenges requiring expert guidance. Neither the author nor the publisher makes any guarantees regarding the results of applying the concepts presented in this book and assume no responsibility for the actions, decisions, or outcomes of readers.

For permissions requests, contact:
contact@ralphclotairejean.com

By reading this book, you acknowledge that you alone are responsible for your choices, decisions, and results.

CONTENTS

To my children—
You are the reason I see the world clearly, the reason I speak the truth boldly, and the reason I walk with purpose every day. Everything in this book is a gift for your future, a shield for your mind, and a light for your path.
May you grow strong, stay awake, and live with courage.
This is for you.
—Ralph Clotaire Jean

To everyone who shaped me—through love, challenge, betrayal, support, honesty, silence, or guidance—thank you.

Every experience sharpened my perception. Every lesson expanded my awareness. Every season prepared me to write this book.

To the people who stood by me, to those who inspired me, and even to those who forced me to grow—your impact lives here, in these pages.

Thank you for being part of my evolution.

FOREWORD

There are books that entertain you,
books that teach you,
and books that pass the time.
This is not one of those books.

My Voice is a guide
for anyone who wants to understand life clearly,
protect their peace,
and walk through the world with purpose and awareness.

Ralph Clotaire Jean has crafted a blueprint—
not to tell you how to live,
but to help you see yourself and the world with uncommon clarity.

This book does not preach.
It awakens.
It does not complicate.
It simplifies.
It does not overwhelm.
It strengthens.

The truths inside these pages are sharp but necessary,
gentle but powerful,
simple but transformative.
If you read with humility,
you will grow.
If you read with courage,
you will evolve.
If you read with honesty,
you will walk away with a deeper understanding of yourself
and the world around you.
This book is more than words—it is a mirror,
a compass,
and a foundation.
You are holding something rare.
Take your time.
Breathe deeply.
And prepare to see life differently.

I wrote this book for anyone who has ever felt lost, confused, overwhelmed, or uncertain about their path in life. I wrote it for the person searching for clarity, truth, strength, purpose, peace, and direction.

I wrote this for the person becoming, not the person pretending.

Every lesson in these pages is carved from lived experience, observation, reflection, and the desire to see clearly in a world that rarely rewards clarity. If you found your way to this book, it means you're ready for something deeper.

My hope is that these words give you courage when life feels heavy, truth when the world feels deceptive, grounding when emotions rise, clarity when everything feels confusing, and strength when you feel alone.

Most of all, I hope this book helps you meet the strongest version of yourself.

Thank you for giving these words a place in your life.

—Ralph Clotaire Jean

PROLOGUE—BEFORE YOU READ ANYTHING

Before you read a single chapter of this book, I want you to pause for a moment and recognize something deeply important:

You are not here by accident. You are here because something inside you is ready to grow.

This book will not tell you who to be. It will not demand that you believe anything. It will not pressure you to accept any worldview.

Instead, this book offers you something rare: truth without fear, guidance without judgment, wisdom without confusion, clarity without complexity.

Every page in this book was written with one intention—to help you understand life clearly, see yourself honestly, and walk through this world with strength, awareness, and purpose.

Before you begin, there is something you must know: Some truths in this book will feel comforting. Some will feel uncomfortable. All of them will help you grow.

Growth is not supposed to feel easy. Awakening is not supposed to feel soft. Transformation is not supposed to feel familiar.

That's why, in this book, you will often be invited to stop and choose: Do you want to keep going? Do you want to learn more? Are you ready for the next level of truth?

Because truth is powerful—and with power comes responsibility.

This book will ask you to see yourself clearly, take accountability, rise above your patterns, build discipline, protect your peace, understand people, strengthen your identity, and step into the life you were meant to live.

Nothing in this book is written to impress you. Everything is written to empower you.

If you read with openness, you will finish this book stronger than you began. If you read with honesty, you will understand yourself in ways most people never reach. If you read with courage, you will walk into the world with clarity that can't be shaken.

Before you start this journey, I want to give you one final truth:

You deserve to know yourself. You deserve to understand this world. You deserve to walk with purpose.

Now—when you are ready, turn the page. Your transformation begins from within.

INTRODUCTION

The world is loud.

People are confused.

Truth is buried beneath distraction, illusion, and noise.

Most people wake up every day and repeat the same patterns—not because they choose to, but because no one ever taught them how life truly works.

This book exists for one reason:

To give you clarity in a world built on confusion.

You will not find complicated theories here.

You will not find empty motivation.

You will not find anything that wastes your time.

Instead, you will find the truths that matter:

How to understand yourself.

How to understand people.

How to protect your energy.

How to build discipline.

How to break patterns.

How to walk with purpose.

How to choose your path.

How to strengthen your identity.

How to build a life with meaning.

Every chapter is designed to be simple, direct, and transformative.

Read slowly.

Reflect deeply.

Return often.

This book is not meant to be read once.

It is meant to be revisited as you grow.

Let your mind be open.

Let your heart be steady.

Let your awareness expand.

Your evolution begins here.

CHAPTER 1—THE WORLD BEHIND THE WORLD

Most people move through life seeing only the surface of things. They react, they guess, they follow, and they repeat. But beneath the surface—beneath the noise and routines—there is a deeper structure to this world, a pattern of truth that only a few ever notice.

You don't learn this in school.

You don't learn it from society.

And you definitely don't learn it from the people who benefit from your silence.

You learn it when you finally stop and ask yourself:

"What is really going on here?"

"Why do people behave the way they do?"

"Why does the world feel like it's designed to distract us?"

The truth is simple:

This world is made of two layers.

The world you see... And the world you're not taught to see.

The world you see is the outer layer—
the rules,
the systems,
the expectations,
the social pressure,
the roles people play.

It's the movies, the news, the trends, the highlights, the illusions.

But the world you're not taught to see is the real one—
human nature,
intention,
insecurity,
ambition,
fear,
desire,
survival,
energy,
influence,
patterns,
truth.

Once you see this deeper layer, you stop being confused by life.
You stop being surprised by people.
You stop taking everything personally.
You stop believing everything at face value.

And you begin to understand:
Life is not random.
People are not unpredictable.
Reality is not chaos.

There are reasons.
There are patterns.

There are motives.

There are invisible forces shaping everything around you.

When you learn to see beneath the surface—

manipulation becomes obvious,

lies become transparent,

intentions become clear,

opportunities become visible,

and you stop wasting time on things that don't matter.

You begin to navigate life with calm, power, and confidence.

You stop living on defense.

You start living on purpose.

The truth is not meant to scare you.

It's meant to free you.

Because once you see the real world—

the world behind the world—

no one can ever blind you again.

This is the beginning of mastery.

CHAPTER 2—THE ILLUSION OF FEAR

F ear is the first wall between you and the life you're meant to live.
Not danger—fear.

Fear is different from danger. Danger is real. Fear is imagined. And most people live their entire lives controlled not by reality, but by their imagination of what could go wrong.

Fear is a storyteller.

It creates movies in your mind about failure, rejection, embarrassment, loss, and judgment.

And the tragedy is this:

Most people never check if the story is true.

They react to every uncomfortable feeling as if it's a warning of disaster.

They run from things that are not threats.

They hide from opportunities that were meant for them.

They avoid people who could have changed their lives.

Fear is the enemy of growth because it's subtle.

It whispers.

It feels like "intuition" when it's actually insecurity.

It feels like "protection" when it's actually limitation.

If you understand this, your entire life changes:

Fear shows up strongest right before your breakthrough.

That nervousness you feel before making a new move is not a signal to stop—

it's a signal that you're standing at the boundary of who you used to be.

Fear only attacks when you're close to becoming more.

People think confident people don't feel fear.

But the truth is:

Confident people feel fear and move anyway.

Weak people feel fear and obey it.

So how do you break free from fear?

You stop asking:

"What if I fail?"

And start asking:

"What if this changes everything?"

You stop asking:

"What if people judge me?"

And start asking:

"What if this is who I was meant to be?"

You stop asking:

"What if I'm not ready?"

And start asking:

"What if I'm more ready than I think?"

Courage is not the absence of fear.

Courage is the decision that something greater than fear is on the other side.

Every major decision in your life will have fear attached to it.

Not because it's dangerous—

but because it's meaningful.

Fear protects the old version of you.

Courage builds the new one.

The moment you realize this, fear loses its power.

It becomes background noise—nothing more.

And once you stop letting fear dictate your choices,

you stop living a small life.

Because the truth is simple:

There is a version of you that fear is terrified of.

Your job is to become that person.

CHAPTER 3—THE POWER OF AWARENESS

Most people go through life half-awake. Their eyes are open, but they're not truly seeing. Their ears work, but they're not actually listening. They hear words, but they miss intentions. They see actions, but they ignore patterns.

Awareness is the skill that separates people who struggle from people who seem to move through life with calm, clarity, and precision.

Awareness is not overthinking, paranoia, or fear. It is simply the ability to recognize what is happening while it's happening.

It is the mental sharpness that allows you to understand who is genuine, who is pretending, what a situation really means, what direction something is heading, what your intuition is telling you, what opportunities are emerging, what dangers are forming, and what your next step should be.

Most people miss what's right in front of them—not because they're weak, but because they're distracted.

Distraction is the real trap of this world.

Not violence.

Not poverty.

Not chaos.

Distraction.

People who lack awareness fall into the same relationships, repeat the same mistakes, trust the wrong people, ignore the right opportunities, react emotionally instead of intelligently, walk into situations blind, and blame "bad luck" instead of noticing patterns.

Awareness turns the lights on.

Once you learn to observe instead of react, everything changes. You begin to ask yourself why this person is saying this, what is really happening here, what the bigger picture is, whether this situation is familiar, what this emotion is trying to tell you, what pattern is repeating, and what the truth is underneath what you're seeing.

Awareness lets you step back and see life the way it truly is, not the way your emotions distort it.

One of the most powerful things awareness reveals is this:

Very few things are personal.

Most things are patterns.

People act based on their insecurities, their upbringing, their fears, their habits, their environment, their unhealed wounds, and their learned survival mechanisms.

It usually has nothing to do with you.

This is why awareness brings peace.

Instead of taking everything personally, you begin to understand:

"Oh... This isn't about me.

This is about who they are."

That one shift alone can save years of frustration.

Awareness is also one of the greatest forms of self-protection.

When you are aware, you see red flags early, you recognize energy shifts, you read rooms, you hear what people don't say, you notice motives and intentions, you feel when something is off, you sense when someone is not who they appear to be, and you avoid traps disguised as opportunities.

Awareness prevents heartbreak.

Awareness prevents betrayal.

Awareness prevents wasted time.

Awareness gives you power—silently, quietly, internally.

You don't need to confront, argue, or expose anything.

You simply understand, adjust, and move wiser.

The moment awareness becomes your default, life stops being confusing.

People stop being unpredictable.

Chaos stops feeling overwhelming.

Because once you see, you can never go back to being blind.

Awareness is the first step to mastery—because you cannot change what you do not notice.

CHAPTER 4—MASTERING YOUR THOUGHTS

Your mind is the battlefield where your future is won or lost. Not the world outside you, not other people, not circumstances—your own thoughts.

Your thoughts shape your decisions, your reactions, your confidence, your habits, your emotions, your relationships, your identity, and your destiny.

Most people think they are thinking—but in reality, their mind is thinking for them. They react to every inner voice automatically. They believe every mental movie without questioning it. They let thoughts pass through their mind like absolute truth, even when the thoughts are lies.

To master your life, you must master your thoughts.

This is not about being positive all the time—that's unrealistic. It's about being in control of the direction your mind points you toward.

Because your mind has two settings:

The mind that protects you.

And the mind that sabotages you.

The protective mind reminds you:

"Stay focused."

"Take the step."

"You can handle this."

"This matters."

"Slow down."

"Think first."

The sabotaging mind whispers:

"You can't."

"What if it fails?"

"They're judging you."

"You're not good enough."

"You should quit."

"Don't try."

The protective mind builds your future.

The sabotaging mind destroys it before it even begins.

Your job is to know which voice is speaking—and to choose the right one.

The key to mastering your thoughts is not to silence the negative voice.

It's to recognize it for what it is:

A survival mechanism, not a truth.

Negative thoughts don't mean you're weak.

They mean your brain is doing its ancient job—trying to protect you from anything uncomfortable or unfamiliar.

But here's the deeper truth:

Your goals and your growth both live outside your comfort zone.

So your brain will resist the very thing you need.

This is why you cannot trust every thought you have.

Your mind will lie to you to keep you safe.

You must learn to respond intelligently instead of automatically.

Here's how:

Observe your thoughts instead of obeying them.

A thought is not a command.

It's just a sentence passing through your mind.

When you hear:

"Don't try."

"It won't work."

"You'll fail."

Step back and say:

"That's just a thought, not the truth."

This alone weakens its power.

Ask: "Does this thought serve my future or my fear?"

Every thought comes from one of two places—your future self or your fearful self.

Future-based thoughts push you forward.

Fear-based thoughts keep you frozen.

Choose the ones that serve your future.

Replace thought reactions with thought decisions.

Don't be reactive.

Be selective.

Ask yourself:

"What is the most useful thought right now?"

"What helps me grow?"

"What supports my direction?"

Then choose that thought deliberately.

Train your mind like a muscle.

Mental strength is built the same way physical strength is built: consistency.

If you constantly choose empowering thoughts over the fearful ones, your brain adapts.

It becomes stronger, sharper, calmer.

Over time, your mind becomes an ally instead of an enemy.

Give your mind a role—or it will create its own.

Tell your mind what to do. Literally.

Every morning:

"Focus."

"Stay disciplined."

"Stay calm."

"Move with purpose."

"Do the hard thing."

Your mind listens more than you think.

If you don't give it instructions, it will default to fear, distraction, and comfort.

Mastering your thoughts does not mean controlling every idea that pops up.

It means mastering your response to those ideas.

Your thoughts are the steering wheel to your life.

If you don't guide them intentionally, they will drift toward the path of least resistance.

And the path of least resistance never leads to greatness.

CHAPTER 5—SEEING THROUGH DECEPTION

One of the most valuable skills you will ever develop is the ability to see what's real—not what's presented to you.

The world is full of masks, narratives, performances, and illusions. People hide their insecurities behind confidence.

They hide their intentions behind kindness.

They hide their motives behind compliments.

They hide their pain behind strength.

They hide their weakness behind loudness.

They hide their emptiness behind success.

And if you take everything at face value, you will misunderstand people, misread situations, and misplace your trust.

Seeing through deception doesn't mean becoming paranoid or cold.

It means becoming aware, wise, and hard to mislead.

Here are the truths you must understand:

People rarely say exactly what they mean.

Words are often softened, filtered, calculated, emotional, defensive, or performative.

To see the truth, watch tone, energy, patterns, consistency, actions, history, and contradictions.

Words are the lowest form of communication.

Patterns are the highest.

People often project their inner world onto the outer world.

When someone is angry for no reason, the reason is inside them.

When someone is jealous or competitive, the insecurity is inside them.

When someone judges you harshly, their judgment is about themselves.

When someone tries to control you, it's because they lack control internally.

Seeing this prevents you from taking things personally.

Most deception is not intentional—it is unconscious.

People lie to themselves before they lie to others.

They deceive themselves about who they are, what they want, what they fear, what they're capable of, what they avoid, how much they hurt, and what they need to change.

Self-deception creates outer deception.

If someone cannot face their own truth, they cannot give you truth either.

Charm is not character.

Some of the most dangerous people in the world are charming.

Charm creates comfort—not honesty.

Never confuse charisma with kindness, confidence with competence, attention with care, flattery with respect, or excitement with compatibility.

Charm wears off.

Character is revealed slowly.

Energy is more honest than words.

A person's energy will tell you if they're genuine, if they're hiding something, if they're jealous, if they're threatened, if they're unstable, if they're trustworthy, if they're manipulating, if they're acting, or if they're real.

Pay attention to how someone makes you feel, not just what they say. Energy never lies.

Deception thrives when you rush. Truth appears when you slow down.

Quick decisions lead to blind spots.

Quick trust leads to disappointment.

Quick judgments lead to confusion.

When you slow down, people reveal themselves, patterns emerge, masks slip, intentions show, and truth rises.

Taking your time is not fear—it's wisdom.

You don't need to expose deception—you just need to stop participating in it.

You do not need to call it out, argue, confront, fight, or prove anything.

Awareness is enough.

When you see someone's truth, you simply adjust your boundaries quietly.

Distance is louder than confrontation.

Silence is stronger than reaction.

Awareness is the ultimate protection.

The greatest deception is the one you tell yourself.

People deceive themselves when they ignore patterns, chase potential instead of reality, excuse disrespect, avoid uncomfortable truths, believe someone's words over their actions, or deny their intuition.

Self-deception is the root of emotional pain.

Clarity begins when you choose truth over comfort.

Seeing through deception doesn't mean becoming cold.

It means becoming clear.

Clarity protects you.

Clarity frees you.

Clarity makes you powerful.

Clarity gives you peace.

Because once you learn to see the real nature of people and situations, you stop living confused—and you start living awake.

CHAPTER 6—DISCIPLINE IS FREEDOM

Most people think discipline is a restriction—a set of rules that takes away comfort, pleasure, or ease.

But the truth is the opposite:

Discipline is the foundation of freedom.

Without discipline, your desires control you.

With discipline, YOU control your life.

People who lack discipline fall into temptation, make emotional decisions, react instead of plan, give up when things get uncomfortable, let fear dictate their choices, start many things and finish nothing, and become slaves to their impulses.

This leads to chaos, regret, and a life with no direction.

But disciplined people live a different reality.

Discipline allows you to build the life you want, stay consistent, stay focused, stay grounded, finish what you start, stay strong under pressure, control your reactions, control your habits, and control your destiny.

The disciplined person and the undisciplined person may have the same fears, the same struggles, and the same setbacks.

But the disciplined person keeps moving.

The undisciplined person keeps stopping.

That is what creates the difference in results.

Discipline is choosing your future over your feelings.

Your feelings say "I'm tired."

"I don't feel like it."

"I'll do it later."

"This is uncomfortable."

"I'm not in the mood."

Your purpose says "Do it anyway."

"Take the next step."

"Stay focused."

"Grow through the discomfort."

"Become who you're meant to be."

Discipline is the bridge between intention and achievement.

Your feelings will never consistently support your goals.

That's why discipline must lead—not emotion.

Discipline protects you from your weaknesses.

Everyone has weaknesses: laziness, fear, distraction, temptation, procrastination, anxiety, self-doubt, emotional reactions.

Discipline builds a structure around you that keeps you from falling into the same traps.

It's not about being perfect—it's about being committed.

Discipline is the cure for inconsistency.

You don't rise to the level of your goals.

You fall to the level of your discipline.

Successful people aren't lucky.

They're consistent.

Consistency creates momentum, confidence, skill, opportunity, health, wealth, and wisdom.

Even if you're not the most talented, disciplined consistency will outperform talent eventually.

Discipline makes your mind stronger than your emotions.

Without discipline, you quit when you're tired, you give up when things get difficult, you react impulsively, and you let discomfort win. With discipline, you push through resistance, you stay focused under pressure, you control your thoughts, and you make decisions from wisdom, not emotion.

You become mentally bulletproof.

Discipline is the highest form of self-respect.

When you discipline yourself, you honor your goals, you honor your standards, you honor your future, you honor your potential, you honor your identity.

You are telling the world:

"I take myself seriously."

People who respect themselves set standards.

People without discipline have no standards—only wishes.

Discipline is not punishment—it is preparation.

Discipline prepares you for challenges, pressure, opportunity, success, leadership, responsibility, unexpected storms.

When you are disciplined, you are always ready.

Life doesn't break disciplined people as easily because they've trained for resistance.

The best time to practice discipline is when you don't feel like it. That moment—when you're tired, annoyed, unmotivated, overwhelmed—is the exact moment discipline builds the most strength.

Every "I don't feel like it" followed by action becomes confidence, resilience, identity, and power.

You stop being the kind of person who starts and quits, and you become the kind of person who finishes.

Discipline is freedom because it makes you unstoppable.

When you are disciplined, you don't depend on motivation, you don't rely on circumstances, you don't wait for the "right moment," you don't need approval, you don't break easily, you don't drift, you don't fear discomfort, and you don't lose control.

You become unstoppable because nothing external can slow someone who has mastered themselves internally.

That is the ultimate freedom.

CHAPTER 7—HUMILITY IS POWER

Humility is one of the most misunderstood qualities in the world.

People often confuse humility with weakness, silence, or softness.

They imagine a humble person as someone who avoids conflict, avoids standing out, or refuses to claim their own strength.

But true humility is the opposite of weakness:

Humility is the ability to stay grounded while becoming great.

Humility is controlled power.

A humble person is not "less than."

A humble person is someone who does not need to prove anything, because they already know who they are.

Humility is strength without arrogance.

Wisdom without ego.

Confidence without noise.

Greatness without the need for attention.

Here are the truths most people never learn:

Humility allows you to grow faster than anyone else.

Arrogant people cannot learn.

They defend their flaws instead of improving them.

They protect their pride instead of strengthening their character.

They try to look right instead of becoming better.

A humble mind says:

"Teach me."

"Show me what I'm missing."

"I can improve."

"There's more to learn."

Humility accelerates growth because it removes resistance to truth.

Humility protects your mind from ego.

Ego ruins everything:

Relationships, careers, opportunities, progress, self-awareness, discipline.

Ego makes you believe you're always right.

Humility makes you understand you can always improve.

Ego destroys potential.

Humility unleashes it.

Humility wins respect—ego demands it.

People might fear ego,

but they respect humility.

Humility attracts mentors, allies, opportunities, trust, support, favor.

Because humble people are easy to teach, easy to work with, and easy to bet on.

Humility is not about lowering yourself.

It's about raising your awareness.

Humility keeps your emotions under control.

Most emotional reactions come from ego:

feeling disrespected, feeling overlooked, feeling offended, feeling challenged, feeling insecure.

Humility lets you respond, not react.

A humble person can say:

"This isn't worth my energy."

"I don't need to prove myself."

"Their opinion doesn't define me."

"I understand the bigger picture."

This gives you emotional freedom.

Humility keeps you wise when life goes well.

Success can blind people.

It can make you careless, arrogant, entitled, reckless, impulsive, disconnected.

Humility keeps your feet on the ground while your mind rises.

It keeps you grateful while you grow.

It keeps you teachable while you succeed.

It keeps you balanced while you elevate.

Humility ensures that success builds you
instead of destroying you.

Humility is magnetic—it draws people closer.

Why?

Because humility makes you safe, trustworthy, grounded, sincere, authentic.

People can rest around someone who is humble.

They don't feel judged.

They don't feel pressured.

They don't feel compared.

They simply feel understood.

And understanding is one of the rarest gifts a person can give.

Humility is the foundation of self-mastery.

Without humility:

You can't learn.

You can't adapt.

You can't grow.

You can't heal.

You can't build deep connections.

You can't see your blind spots.

Humility keeps you honest with yourself.

It lets you say:

"I was wrong."

"I need to improve this."

"I'm still learning."

"I can do better."

These statements don't weaken you—

they strengthen you faster than anything else.

Humility is power because it removes the need to pretend.

Pretending is exhausting:

Pretending to be right,

pretending to know everything,

pretending you're not hurt,

pretending you're not insecure,

pretending you're above correction,

pretending you're fine when you're not.

Humility lets you breathe.

Humility lets you be real.

Humility lets you evolve.

When you stop performing for the world,

you finally start becoming who you were meant to be.

And that is the greatest power of all.

CHAPTER 8—COURAGE IS A DAILY CHOICE

People imagine courage as a single moment—a dramatic decision, a great act of bravery, a leap into the unknown.

But true courage is not a moment.

It is a daily practice.

Courage is waking up and choosing:

Discipline over comfort.

Honesty over avoidance.

Self-respect over approval.

Purpose over fear.

Growth over excuses.

No one becomes courageous overnight.

Courage grows every time you make a decision that your fear disagrees with.

Here's what most people don't understand:

Courage is not the absence of fear.

Courage is acting in spite of it.

Fear says: "Stay where you are."

Courage says: "Move anyway."

Fear says: "What if you fail?"

Courage says: "What if this works?"

Fear says: "What will they think?"

Courage says: "What do I think?"

Fear protects you from imagined threats.

Courage leads you toward real transformation.

Courage is doing what you know is right—even when it's uncomfortable.

The hardest decisions in life are usually the right ones:

Walking away from people who drain you.

Cutting off habits that destroy you.

Saying no when it's easier to say yes.

Telling the truth.

Starting over.

Leaving comfort behind.

Putting yourself first.

Committing to change.

These choices require courage because they force you to confront the real you.

Growth is uncomfortable.

Healing is uncomfortable.

Discipline is uncomfortable.

But so is staying stuck.

Choose your discomfort wisely.

Courage is facing yourself honestly.

You cannot heal what you refuse to face.

You cannot grow beyond what you deny.

You cannot fix what you won't acknowledge.

It takes courage to say:

"I was wrong."

"I need to change."

"I haven't been giving my best."

"I've been avoiding this."

"I created some of my own problems."

This level of honesty makes people powerful, not broken.

Courage is letting go of who you used to be.

Most people stay stuck because they stay loyal to an outdated identity:

Old habits.

Old beliefs.

Old patterns.

Old environments.

Old versions of themselves.

They are more committed to their past than their future.

Courage is saying:

"I'm ready to evolve."

You are allowed to:

Outgrow people.

Outgrow environments.

Outgrow expectations.

Outgrow the version of you that others knew.

Outgrow who you once were.

This is not betrayal.

This is growth.

Courage is showing up even when you feel unprepared.

No one ever feels "ready."

Readiness is not a feeling—it's a decision.

You don't wait for confidence to appear.

You build confidence by showing up.

You don't wait for fear to disappear.

You move through fear until it becomes smaller.

You don't wait for perfect conditions.

You create momentum by acting now.

Success belongs to the people who show up,

not the people who wait for permission.

Courage is being different in a world that wants you to be the same.

Society pressures people to:

Fit in.

Stay quiet.

Avoid risk.

Follow the crowd.

Live for approval.

Suppress individuality.

It takes courage to:

Think for yourself.

Stand alone.

Reject the herd.

Choose your own direction.

Speak the truth.

Live by your own values.

Most people fear standing out because they fear judgment.

But judgment fades.

Regret lasts.

Courage is a muscle—you strengthen it by using it.

Every courageous act, no matter how small, builds the next one.

Courage grows when you:

Make the call.

Send the message.

Start the project.

Set the boundary.

Have the conversation.

Take the risk.

Choose the hard thing.

Each act becomes a brick in the foundation of your character.

Over time, you become someone who moves through life with quiet, powerful confidence.

Courage makes you unstoppable because it removes the limits fear places around your life.

Fear shrinks your world.

Courage expands it.

The life you want—the relationships, the growth, the opportunities, the peace, the strength—

all live on the other side of the decisions you're afraid to make.

Courage doesn't guarantee success.

But it guarantees transformation.

And transformed people transform their lives.

CHAPTER 9—REPROGRAMMING THE MIND

Your mind is powerful, but it is also programmable.

Everything you've experienced—family, school, culture, pain, wins, losses, fear, society—has shaped the way you think.

And most people never question the programming they inherited.

They don't ask:

Why do I think like this?

Where did this belief come from?

Does this mindset help me or limit me?

Is this fear even mine, or did I learn it from someone else?

The truth is simple:

You were programmed before you were conscious enough to choose.

Now it's your responsibility to reprogram yourself intentionally.

Your mind is not your identity.

It is software.

You can update it.

You can rewrite it.

You can remove what no longer serves you.

You can build new beliefs that match the life you want—not the life you were taught to expect.

Your old programming was built for survival, not success.

Most people were raised to stay safe, avoid discomfort, be agreeable, fear judgment, settle for what's available, follow the crowd, prioritize approval, minimize risk, think small, and avoid standing out.

This programming helps you survive,

but it prevents you from growing.

To change your life, you must change the default settings in your mind.

Question everything you believe.

Every belief you hold should be examined:

Where did this belief come from?

Who taught it to me?

Did I choose this, or was it placed on me?

Does this belief help me become stronger, or weaker?

Most of the beliefs that limit you are inherited, not chosen.

Reprogramming begins with one powerful decision:

Stop letting old programming run your new life.

Replace self-limiting thoughts with self-directed ones.

Your mind will always offer you the predictable, comfortable, safe thought.

You must replace it deliberately.

Instead of: "I can't."

Say: "I can learn."

Instead of: "What if I fail?"

Say: "What if this works?"

Instead of: "This is too hard."

Say: "This is how I grow stronger."

Instead of: "I'm not ready."

Say: "I'll start and learn as I go."

Your thoughts shape your identity.

Your identity shapes your actions.

Your actions shape your life.

If you want a new life, start with new thoughts.

Build mental habits that support the future you want.

To reprogram your mind, you need daily habits that reinforce your new identity:

Reading.

Journaling.

Meditation.

Learning.

Self-reflection.

Intentional silence.

Setting goals.

Keeping promises to yourself.

Spending time around elevated people.

Cutting off mental poison.

Small habits change your psychology.

Your psychology changes your life.

Surround yourself with people who stretch your mind.

Your environment is the most powerful programmer of all.

If you surround yourself with people who think small, complain, fear change, avoid growth, or settle for less,

your mind will adapt to that level.

But if you surround yourself with people who think big, aim high,
take risks, speak truth, value self-growth, and chase purpose,
your mind will stretch to match them.

Your environment sets your mental ceiling.

Replace emotional reactions with conscious responses.
Old programming reacts.
New programming responds.

When you feel anger, fear, anxiety, insecurity, jealousy, or frustration,
pause and ask:
Is this emotion coming from the present moment, or from old programming?

Most emotional reactions come from the past, not the present.
Reprogramming lets you respond intelligently instead of emotionally.

Rewrite the story you tell yourself.
Your internal narrative becomes your fate.

If your story is:
"I'm unlucky."
"People always hurt me."
"I never succeed."
"I'm not good enough."
"Nothing ever works out for me."
Your life will match that story.

But if your story becomes:
"I'm capable."
"I'm learning."
"I'm disciplined."
"I'm evolving."
"I'm stronger than my past."
"I create opportunities."

"I am becoming who I was meant to be."
Your life will match that story too.

The story you repeat becomes the identity you accept.
The identity you accept becomes the life you live.
Rewrite the story.
Rewrite the mind.
Rewrite the life.

Reprogramming doesn't make life easy—it makes you powerful.
Life will always bring pressure, challenges, setbacks, uncertainty, and unexpected situations.
But a reprogrammed mind stays calm, stays focused, stays grounded, stays disciplined, and stays resilient.

The world doesn't get easier.
You get stronger.
And the stronger you become internally,
the freer you become externally.

This is the essence of a powerful life.

CHAPTER 10—BECOMING EMOTIONALLY UNTOUCHABLE

Most people live as prisoners of their emotions.

They are controlled by what they feel in the moment:

Anger.

Fear.

Insecurity.

Jealousy.

Impulsiveness.

Anxiety.

Hurt.

Confusion.

When emotions are in control, your reactions become automatic, not intelligent.

You say things you don't mean.

You make decisions you later regret.

You let temporary feelings sabotage long-term goals.

Emotional mastery is not about feeling nothing.

It's about not letting feelings control your behavior.

This is what it means to become emotionally untouchable:

You feel everything, but you are controlled by nothing.

You stop reacting automatically and start responding intentionally.

This single skill can change your entire life.

Emotional triggers are teachers, not enemies.

Every strong emotion you feel is a message.

Anger means a boundary was crossed.

Jealousy means there is something you desire that you're not pursuing.

Fear means you're approaching growth.

Anxiety means you're thinking about the future instead of the present.

Sadness means something needs to be processed.

Instead of running from emotions, study them.

Understanding your emotional patterns is how you break them.

Pause before reacting.

Reacting instantly is how you destroy relationships, opportunities, and peace.

The pause is powerful.

When something upsets you:

Stop.

Breathe.

Observe the emotion.

Let the intensity fall.

Then choose your response.

This prevents most unnecessary conflict.

A one-second pause can save you years of regret.

Don't let people control you with their energy.

People try to pull you into their anger, their drama, their insecurity, their chaos, their emotional storms.

When you stay calm, you refuse to join their emotional world.

This is how you maintain your power.

Never match someone's dysfunction.

Hold your own frequency.

A calm person is always stronger than a reactive one.

Detach from things you cannot control.

Most emotional pain comes from trying to control people, outcomes, timing, opinions, the past, or unfair situations.

Emotional mastery is the ability to say:

"I release everything that is not mine to hold."

Focus only on your effort, your character, your response, your standards, your peace.

Everything else is noise.

Do not chase validation.

One of the fastest ways to lose emotional strength is to depend on approval, attention, reassurance, applause, or compliments.

When your worth is external, you become emotionally fragile.

But when your worth comes from discipline, growth, purpose, truth, and self-respect,

you become emotionally unshakeable.

People can reject you, misunderstand you, or overlook you—
and you still remain whole.

Take nothing personally.

People's reactions are rarely about you.

They are about their wounds, their fears, their insecurities, their stress, their internal conflict, their assumptions, their worldview.

When you realize this, you stop being offended by everything.

Emotional freedom begins when you understand:

"This is not about me."

Master your internal dialogue.

Your emotions follow your thoughts.

If you think:

"They're judging me."

"I'm not good enough."

"I always mess up."

Your emotions will mirror that.

But if you think:

"I am capable."

"I am evolving."

"I can handle this."

"I'm improving every day."

Your emotions shift accordingly.

Change the thought → change the emotion.

This is emotional mastery at its core.

Respond from wisdom, not wounds.

Many people live through emotional wounds they've never healed.

So they react from abandonment, fear, past trauma, childhood conditioning, insecurity, mistrust, and betrayal.

Becoming emotionally untouchable means healing what once controlled you.

Heal the wound, and the reaction loses its power.

Emotional strength makes you a stable force in an unstable world.

Most people are ruled by impulses.

A few are ruled by logic.

But the rarest people are those who are ruled by wisdom.

When you become calm, centered, grounded, intentional, and emotionally disciplined,

you become someone others trust, someone others respect, someone others rely on.

Your presence becomes strength.

Emotional mastery is a lifelong practice.

You don't become emotionally untouchable in a day.

It's built through daily awareness, daily discipline, daily self-control, and daily introspection.

But over time, something incredible happens:

You stop being shaken by small things.

You stop being distracted by chaos.

You stop being manipulated by emotions.

You stop losing control.

You stop being pulled into other people's storms.

You become the calm within the storm.

This is the power of emotional mastery.

CHAPTER 11—THE LAWS OF GROWTH

G rowth is not an accident.
It is not luck, talent, timing, or chance.
Growth follows laws—laws that apply to everyone, regardless of background, personality, or circumstances.

When you understand these laws, life becomes clearer.
Barriers feel smaller.
Challenges feel purposeful.
Progress feels predictable.

The laws of growth explain why some people evolve rapidly while others stay the same for years.

Here are the truths every powerful person eventually discovers.

Growth begins where comfort ends.
If your life feels comfortable, predictable, and effortless,
you are not growing—you are maintaining.

Growth requires discomfort, new experiences, risk, uncertainty, difficulty, change, and pressure.

Comfort feels safe,
but nothing grows in safety.
    A plant cannot grow in a sealed glass box.
It needs light, air, and weather—even harsh weather.
The same is true for you.
    Growth requires honesty.
Honesty with yourself is the first step:
What patterns are holding me back?
What habits are hurting me?
What lies have I been telling myself?
What weaknesses have I ignored?
What fears am I avoiding?
What excuses have I normalized?
    Most people avoid these questions,
which is why most people repeat the same year of life over and over.
Growth demands truth—even when it's uncomfortable.
    Growth is not linear—it comes in waves.
You will experience breakthroughs, plateaus, setbacks, frustration,
rapid progress, slow progress, moments of doubt, and moments of
clarity.
This is normal.
    A seed takes time before anything appears above the soil.
A tree roots downward before it grows upward.
Just because you can't see progress
doesn't mean progress isn't happening.
    Consistency always pays off—but not always immediately.
    Growth requires letting go of the old you.
You cannot become the next version of yourself
while clinging to the last one.

You must let go of old beliefs, old habits, old stories, old identities, old relationships, old environments, and old versions of yourself.

Growth feels like loss at first
because you must release what is familiar
to gain what is possible.
This is why growth requires courage.

Growth requires friction.
Pressure shapes you.
Resistance strengthens you.
Challenges refine you.

A muscle grows only by being torn and rebuilt.
The mind grows the same way.

Every challenge you face has a purpose:
Frustration builds patience.
Failure builds strategy.
Heartbreak builds wisdom.
Fear builds courage.
Disappointment builds resilience.

Life does not give you pain to destroy you—
it gives you pain to teach you.

Growth requires consistency, not perfection.
You don't need to be perfect to grow.
You just need to keep going.

Growth is built in small, repeated actions:
Reading daily.
Exercising regularly.
Thinking intentionally.
Practicing discipline.
Speaking truth.

Showing up.

Trying again.

Perfection is a trap.

Consistency is a path.

Aim for progress, not perfection.

Growth requires humility.

You cannot grow if you think you already know everything.

Humility lets you learn from others, receive correction, see blind spots, stay adaptable, ask for guidance, and drop your ego.

Humility isn't weakness—

humility is openness.

An open mind evolves.

A closed mind repeats.

Growth requires environment.

Your environment is stronger than your willpower.

If you surround yourself with comfort, negativity, gossip, stagnation, excuses, and distraction,

your growth will suffocate.

But if you surround yourself with ambition, discipline, truth, accountability, high standards, and vision,

your growth will accelerate.

Environment is not just where you live—

it's what you consume, who you spend time with, and what you tolerate.

Growth requires identity shift.

Long-term growth becomes natural

when your identity matches your goals.

Instead of saying:

"I want to be disciplined,"

you say:

"I am disciplined."

    Instead of saying:

"I hope I improve,"

you say:

"I improve every day."

    Your actions will always follow your identity.

Become the person your goals require.

    Growth is a lifelong process.

You don't arrive.

You evolve.

Then you evolve again.

And again.

    The moment you think you're done growing

is the moment you start declining.

    Growth keeps you alive internally.

Growth keeps you young mentally.

Growth keeps you expanding spiritually.

Growth keeps you aligned with your highest potential.

    Growth isn't something you chase—

it's something you choose.

And the choice must be made daily.

CHAPTER 12—PAIN AS YOUR TEACHER

Most people fear pain.

They run from it, avoid it, numb it, deny it, and distract themselves from it.

But pain is not your enemy.

Pain is a messenger.

Pain is a guide.

Pain is a mirror.

Pain is a mentor.

Pain shows you what needs to change, what needs to heal, and what needs to be released.

Nothing transforms you faster than discomfort—
not success, not praise, not pleasure, not motivation.

Pain forces honesty.

Pain forces growth.

Pain forces evolution.

Here are the deeper truths.

Pain exposes what comfort hides.

Comfort can hide weakness, fear, insecurity, broken habits, poor decisions, denial, unhealthy relationships, and emotional wounds.

Pain exposes them instantly.

When something hurts, it's revealing a truth that comfort was covering.

This is why pain is valuable.

Pain shows you what you must let go of.

Sometimes pain doesn't come to ruin your life—

it comes to remove something that would have ruined you later.

Pain tells you:

"This person is not meant for your future."

"This pattern is destroying you."

"This belief is limiting you."

"This environment no longer matches you."

"This version of you can't take you where you're going."

Pain clears the path for your evolution.

Pain strengthens you in ways ease cannot.

Ease teaches nothing.

Discomfort teaches everything.

Pain builds resilience, patience, wisdom, discipline, courage, emotional strength, and clarity.

A person who has never struggled often remains fragile.

A person who has faced pain consciously becomes unbreakable.

Pain forces you to confront truth.

We often avoid truth because truth demands change.

But pain makes avoidance impossible.

Pain says:

"Look at this."

"Acknowledge this."

"Deal with this."

"Heal this."

"Outgrow this."

Pain is not cruelty.

Pain is clarity.

Pain teaches you what matters.

Pain strips your life down to the essential.

It shows you who truly cares, what truly matters, what was never real, what you've been ignoring, and what your soul actually needs.

Pain removes illusions.

It reconnects you with what is real.

Pain humbles you.

Pain reminds you that you are human, you are learning, you have limits, you have blind spots, and you must evolve.

This humility becomes inner strength.

A humble person learns faster.

A humble person adapts quicker.

A humble person grows deeper.

Pain softens the ego but strengthens the spirit.

Pain gives birth to wisdom.

Most wisdom is earned, not learned.

Books can educate you.

Teachers can guide you.

Life can instruct you.

But pain engraves truth into your soul.

Some lessons are only available through experience:

Heartbreak.

Disappointment.

Betrayal.

Loss.

Failure.

Rejection.

Mistakes.

These experiences open your eyes in ways nothing else can.

Pain prepares you for the next level of your life.

Growth requires strength.

Strength requires resistance.

Resistance requires discomfort.

Every painful experience is preparing you for a future version of yourself.

Pain is the universe sharpening your character.

When something hurts deeply, it is often because something deep is being reshaped.

Pain is temporary, but its lessons are permanent.

The intensity fades.

The tears dry.

The anger dissolves.

The confusion clears.

But the lesson—

the growth—

the wisdom—

the transformation—

they stay with you forever.

Pain passes.

Progress remains.

Pain becomes power once you understand it.

People who have never faced their pain avoid life.

People who have faced their pain master life.

When you stop fearing discomfort:

You become courageous.

You take risks.

You set boundaries.

You speak truth.

You chase purpose.

You stop settling.

You rise higher.

    Pain wakes you up.

Pain pushes you forward.

Pain breaks you open so you can rebuild yourself stronger.

    You don't grow when life is easy.

You grow when life challenges you.

CHAPTER 13—BREAKING OLD PATTERNS

Your life doesn't change because you want it to.

Your life changes because you interrupt the patterns that have been quietly running your behavior for years.

Patterns decide who you love, who you trust, what you avoid, what you chase, how you handle stress, how you react, how you think, and what you believe you deserve.

Most people aren't controlled by outside forces.
They're controlled by cycles they don't notice.

Breaking old patterns is one of the hardest things you'll ever do—and one of the most liberating.

It requires honesty, awareness, courage, and a willingness to choose differently even when you're uncomfortable.

Here are the truths every person must face.

Patterns repeat until you learn the lesson.

Life has a way of sending the same type of person, challenge, conflict, disappointment, temptation, or situation over and over, until you finally respond differently.

If you keep attracting the same experiences, it's not coincidence— it's a pattern asking to be broken.

Patterns are teachers.

When you evolve, the pattern ends.

Your subconscious habits run more of your life than your conscious decisions.

Most of your behavior is automatic—how you handle rejection, how you cope with stress, how you communicate, how you set boundaries, how you react emotionally, how you deal with conflict, how you deal with fear.

These are not conscious choices— these are learned scripts.

Breaking patterns requires becoming conscious of what used to be automatic.

Once you notice the script, you can rewrite it.

You cannot break a pattern you deny.

Denial keeps cycles alive.

People say:

"I'm fine."

"It's not that bad."

"I don't care."

"This is just who I am."

"That's just how life is."

These phrases keep you trapped.

Patterns end when you tell the truth:

"This relationship is draining me."

"This habit is holding me back."

"This belief isn't mine anymore."

"I keep repeating this mistake."

"I need to change this."

Honesty is disruption.

Disruption is transformation.

You outgrow patterns when you outgrow the version of yourself that created them.

Patterns are not random—they match your identity.

If your identity is "I always get hurt," you stop choosing safe people.

If your identity is "I'm not disciplined," you stop choosing discipline.

If your identity is "I'm not meant for more," you stop reaching.

When you change your identity,

your patterns no longer fit you.

You cannot live a new life with an old identity.

Emotional triggers reveal your patterns.

Every strong emotional reaction is a clue.

If you want to understand your patterns, examine what triggers you:

What makes you angry?

What makes you insecure?

What makes you jealous?

What makes you shut down?

What makes you overreact?

What makes you chase?

What makes you avoid?

Triggers show you where you were wounded, where you were conditioned, where you have not healed, and where your patterns began.

Your triggers tell the story of your past

and point the direction of your healing.

Breaking patterns requires choosing the uncomfortable option.
Your mind will always push you back toward the familiar because the
familiar feels safe—even when it's harmful.

To break patterns, you must choose the opposite response.
You must choose the healthier boundary.
You must choose the honest conversation.
You must choose the calm reaction.
You must choose the different decision.
You must choose the higher standard.
You must choose the new environment.

Growth feels awkward at first
because it contradicts everything your old self normalized.
But that discomfort is the signal of transformation.

Patterns often come from childhood—but they end in adulthood.
Many of your adult behaviors are coping mechanisms you learned as
a child:

Pleasing people to avoid conflict.
Staying silent to stay safe.
Overworking to feel worthy.
Shutting down to protect yourself.
Chasing validation to feel loved.

These patterns made sense then.
They do not serve you now.

You cannot control who you were forced to be as a child,
but you can choose who you become as an adult.
That choice breaks generational cycles.

You don't break patterns with willpower—you break them with
awareness.
Willpower fades.
Awareness shifts reality.

Once you truly see a pattern,

you can't unsee it.

It no longer feels normal.

It no longer feels acceptable.

It no longer feels like "you."

Your mind begins to resist the old behavior.

Awareness disrupts autopilot.

Awareness rewrites the script.

Awareness changes your life.

Surrounding yourself with a new environment accelerates new patterns.

Your environment influences your habits, your beliefs, your standards, and your identity.

If you stay around people who reinforce your old patterns,

you will slip back into them.

But when you surround yourself with people who think higher, live healthier, move with purpose, challenge you, inspire you, and grow consistently,

your new patterns become natural.

Environment is activation.

Breaking patterns is not a one-time event—it's a lifestyle.

You don't break a pattern and walk away forever.

You break it every day until your new identity becomes your default.

Over time, what once was difficult becomes effortless.

What once was unconscious becomes intentional.

What once was a cycle becomes a memory.

The moment you break your patterns, you reclaim your power.

And when you reclaim your power,

your life becomes yours again.

CHAPTER 14—THE TRUTH ABOUT PURPOSE

Purpose is one of the most misunderstood concepts in life.

People imagine purpose as a single mission, a grand calling, or some mysterious destiny waiting to be discovered.

They think purpose is hidden somewhere far away, and that one day it will suddenly reveal itself.

But the truth is this:

Purpose is not something you find.

Purpose is something you build.

It grows as you grow.

It expands as you expand.

It becomes clearer as you become clearer.

Purpose is a byproduct of alignment—

alignment with who you truly are, what you value, and what you're becoming.

Here are the truths most people never realize.

Purpose is created through action, not thought.

You cannot think your way into purpose.

You discover it through movement.

Purpose reveals itself when you try new things, fail, learn, improve, explore, experiment, pay attention, and stay open.

Purpose grows through experience, not imagination.

You won't find purpose by waiting.

You'll find it by living.

Purpose begins with contribution.

Purpose is rooted in impact.

Ask yourself:

What do I give?

Who do I help?

What do I make better?

What value do I create?

What does the world gain through me?

Purpose is not about being important.

Purpose is about being useful.

When your life improves the lives of others, you are living with purpose.

Purpose evolves with each chapter of your life.

The purpose you had at fifteen is not the purpose you have at twenty-five.

The purpose you have at twenty-five won't be the same as the purpose you have at forty-five.

Each season of life has its own mission:

Learning.

Healing.

Growing.

Building.

Serving.

Leading.

Teaching.

Guiding.

Purpose is not a destination.

Purpose is a direction.

Purpose is connected to what strengthens you, not just what excites you.

Excitement fades.

Strength remains.

You may be excited about many things,
but purpose aligns with what you can sustain, what you can endure, what you can commit to, what challenges you grow from, what deepens your character, and what builds your discipline.

Purpose requires responsibility, not just passion.

Purpose is usually found where pain was.
Your deepest wounds often reveal your greatest calling.

Pain shapes compassion.

Pain shapes wisdom.

Pain shapes strength.

Pain shapes direction.

The experiences that nearly broke you
are often the experiences that prepare you
to help others, solve problems, or bring truth into the world.

Your purpose often lies in the very place you once struggled.

Purpose requires sacrifice.
You cannot live with purpose and live comfortably at the same time.

Purpose demands discipline, effort, consistency, responsibility, courage, growth, and accountability.

Purpose will ask you to rise above your excuses.

It will ask you to leave behind distractions.

It will ask you to choose growth over comfort.

Purpose is not easy.

But it is meaningful.

Purpose is not a job—it is a way of living.

Your job may change.

Your environment may change.

Your relationships may change.

But your purpose comes from within.

Purpose is how you show up:

Your integrity.

Your discipline.

Your character.

Your energy.

Your standards.

Your presence.

Your contribution.

Purpose is who you become, not just what you do.

Purpose requires alignment, not approval.

You cannot live on purpose while living for validation.

Purpose is often misunderstood by friends, family, society, coworkers, people who think small, people who fear change, and people who don't see your vision.

You must be willing to walk alone sometimes.

Purpose requires self-trust.

Purpose gives your life clarity, strength, and direction.

When you live with purpose,

you stop chasing meaningless things.

You stop overreacting.

You stop comparing.

You stop seeking distractions.

You stop feeling lost.

You stop living on autopilot.

Purpose gives you focus, meaning, discipline, patience, resilience, and peace.

Purpose is fuel.

Purpose is your responsibility.

No one can give you your purpose.

No one can tell you your purpose.

No one can walk your purpose for you.

You must choose it.

You must build it.

You must commit to it.

You must honor it.

Purpose is the path you carve through life with intention.

Your purpose is not out there waiting.

It is in here, growing with every step you take.

CHAPTER 15—BUILDING A POWERFUL IDENTITY

Your identity is the foundation of everything you do in life. It is the internal blueprint that shapes your thoughts, behavior, habits, and decisions.

Nothing influences your future more than the identity you accept.

Here's the truth:

You don't rise to the level of your goals.

You rise to the level of your identity.

If your identity is small, your actions will be small.

If your identity is strong, your actions will be strong.

Your identity sets your standards, and your standards shape your life.

Identity is not who you are—it's who you *decide* to be.

You are not limited by your past, your mistakes, your upbringing, your environment, your fears, or your history.

Identity is not inherited.

Identity is chosen.

You can shift your identity at any moment by saying:

"I am becoming the person my future requires."

You stop saying:

"I am stuck."

And start saying:

"I am evolving."

The moment you choose a higher identity, your behavior follows.

Your identity is built by your daily habits.

Your habits tell you who you really are.

If you want to know your current identity, ask yourself:

What do I do consistently?

What do I tolerate?

What do I avoid?

What do I prioritize?

What do I finish?

What do I abandon?

What excuses do I repeat?

Your identity is not formed by big moments.

It is formed by small, repeated behaviors.

A powerful identity requires powerful habits.

Stop identifying with your weaknesses.

Many people unconsciously build identities around their limitations.

These are not identities—they are wounds.

And wounds should not define your life.

A powerful identity starts with powerful statements:

"I am disciplined."

"I am focused."

"I am growing."

"I am learning."

"I am becoming stronger."

"I am capable."

You stop saying:

"I'm broken."

And start saying:

"I'm rebuilding."

You become what you repeatedly say about yourself.

Your identity must match your future, not your past.

Your past version of yourself didn't have the wisdom, discipline, self-awareness, or inner strength you have now.

Do not let a former version of yourself define your present.

You owe loyalty to your future, not your past.

Your identity is shaped by the standards you refuse to lower.

Standards protect your identity.

Your standards determine who you allow access to, what behavior you tolerate, how you treat yourself, how you let people treat you, what work you accept, what environments you stay in, and what you say yes or no to.

Low standards destroy high potential.

High standards create a high identity.

Discipline builds the identity that confidence depends on.

Confidence is not a personality trait.

Confidence is the side effect of keeping promises to yourself.

People who lack confidence don't lack ability—they lack proof.

When you stay disciplined, you trust yourself, you respect yourself, you believe in yourself, you depend on yourself, and you stop seeking validation.

Discipline builds identity.

Identity builds confidence.

Identity grows from challenges, not comfort.

Every challenge you overcome strengthens your identity.

Every time you don't quit, every time you control your emotions, every time you choose discipline, every time you walk away from disrespect, every time you build instead of complain, every time you improve instead of avoid, every time you face fear, every time you choose the higher path—

you become someone stronger.

A strong identity is forged, not found.

Protect your identity from environments that weaken it.

Your identity is shaped by the people you talk to, the rooms you walk into, the content you consume, and the energy you surround yourself with.

If your environment contradicts your identity, your identity will collapse.

If your environment supports your identity, your identity will thrive.

Choose your environments wisely.

Identity is not loud—it's steady.

People who scream their identity haven't built one.

True identity is quiet.

It speaks through consistency, action, presence, character, boundaries, and discipline.

A powerful identity does not need to be announced.

It is obvious.

You become unstoppable when your identity aligns with your purpose.

When your identity aligns with your purpose, you stop forcing discipline.

Your behavior becomes natural.

You no longer need motivation.

You don't negotiate with excuses.

You don't doubt yourself.

You don't question your path.

You don't break under pressure.

    You simply live as the person you were meant to become.

    Identity is destiny.

Build it deliberately.

Protect it fiercely.

Grow it continuously.

CHAPTER 16—PROTECTING YOUR ENERGY

Your energy is one of the most valuable resources you possess.

It influences your thoughts, decisions, mood, relationships, focus, discipline, and the direction of your entire life.

When your energy is protected, you move through the world with clarity and power.

When your energy is drained, you become reactive, scattered, and disconnected from your purpose.

Protecting your energy isn't selfish.

It's essential.

Here are the truths you must master.

Not everyone deserves access to you.

Some people add to your energy.

Others drain it.

Some elevate you.

Others distract you.

Some inspire growth.

Others pull you into cycles you've already outgrown.

Your peace is your responsibility.

You don't need to hate anyone to set boundaries.

You don't need to argue to create distance.

You don't need to justify protecting your sanity.

Your energy is not public property.

Protect your energy by choosing silence over chaos.

Not everything deserves a reaction.

Not every insult deserves a defense.

Not every argument deserves your presence.

Not every invitation deserves your time.

Silence is not weakness.

Silence is strategy.

When you stay silent, you stay in control.

You save your energy.

You keep your dignity.

You avoid unnecessary conflict.

You protect your peace.

Noise is cheap.

Silence is power.

Protect your energy by setting firm boundaries.

Boundaries are not restrictions—they are filters.

They protect your mental health, your time, your focus, your goals, and your self-respect.

Boundaries tell the world:

"This is where my peace ends and your behavior begins."

If someone cannot respect your boundaries,

they are not meant for your future.

Protect your energy by controlling who influences you.

You absorb the mindset of the people you spend time with.

If you surround yourself with negativity, gossip, laziness, fear, jealousy, drama, excuses—

you will absorb that energy.

But if you surround yourself with discipline, purpose, truth, ambition, clarity, peace, and high standards—

you will rise without effort.

Your circle shapes your energy.

Your energy shapes your life.

Protect your energy by honoring your limits.

Pushing yourself is good.

Destroying yourself is not.

You must learn to recognize when you need rest, solitude, reflection, reset, quiet, and space.

There is strength in knowing when to pull back.

There is wisdom in knowing when to pause.

Rest is not laziness.

Rest is preparation.

Protect your energy by not taking things personally.

People don't act based on who you are.

They act based on who they are—

their wounds, their fears, their traumas, their conditioning, their insecurities.

Understanding this saves you from unnecessary emotional storms.

Nothing is more energy-draining than carrying burdens that don't belong to you.

Release the need to take everything personally.

You will feel lighter instantly.

Protect your energy by staying aligned with your purpose.

Distractions weaken you.

Purpose strengthens you.

The more aligned you are with your purpose:

The less drama affects you.

The less pettiness tempts you.

The less negativity pulls you in.

The less chaos you tolerate.

Purpose gives you tunnel vision.

It sharpens your priorities.

It filters out noise.

When your life has direction, you become immune to distraction.

Protect your energy by avoiding emotional entanglements.

Some people thrive on conflict, chaos, manipulation, attention, and control.

Do not let them pull you into their storms.

The person who controls your emotions controls you.

Stay calm.

Stay grounded.

Stay detached.

You don't have to participate in every emotional invitation.

Protect your energy by choosing peace—even when you're right.

Winning arguments is meaningless.

Winning your peace is priceless.

You don't need to prove yourself.

You don't need validation.

You don't need the last word.

You don't need to be understood by everyone.

Peace over ego.

Always.

Protect your energy by building a lifestyle that supports your well-being.

Your energy is shaped by what you do daily:

Sleep, diet, movement, self-talk, habits, environment, routine, discipline.

A strong lifestyle creates strong energy.

Disorder weakens you.

Structure strengthens you.

Protect your energy the way a king protects his kingdom.

Because your energy determines the quality of your entire life.

CHAPTER 17—DEALING WITH PEOPLE AND THEIR INTENTIONS

Understanding people is one of the most important life skills you can ever master.

Not to judge them, but to navigate life with clarity instead of confusion.

Most of the stress people experience comes from misunderstanding:

Who people are, what they want, what they're capable of, and what role they should play in your life.

The truth is simple:

People reveal themselves through patterns, not moments.

If you learn to see people clearly, you will avoid most unnecessary pain.

Here are the truths that will protect you.

People act from their character, not your value.

You can be loyal, honest, loving, supportive, and genuine—

and someone can still lie to you, mistreat you, or take you for granted.

Why?

Because their actions are based on their maturity, their wounds, their intentions, their fears, their morals, their discipline, their inner world.

You cannot control someone's character.

You can only choose your proximity to it.

Pay attention to patterns, not apologies.

People can apologize endlessly.

Words are cheap.

Consistency reveals sincerity.

Do they apologize but repeat the behavior?

Do they promise change but avoid accountability?

Do they take responsibility or make excuses?

Do they improve or stay the same?

Strong people change patterns.

Weak people change stories.

Not every person in your life is meant to stay.

Some people are seasonal.

They come into your life to teach you lessons, boundaries, self-respect, direction, clarity, strength.

Once the lesson is complete, the relationship often fades.

This is not failure.

This is transition.

Your life is a journey with chapters.

Some people belong in earlier chapters, not the next ones.

Protect yourself from people who drain your energy.

There are people who take more than they give, complain more than they act, need attention more than they offer support, demand energy but give none back, depend on you emotionally but never lift you up, create chaos and call it your responsibility.

These people do not need punishment.

They need distance.

Your peace is more important than someone's access to you.

Listen to how people talk about others.

How someone talks about others is how they will eventually talk about you.

Do they gossip?

Do they judge people harshly?

Do they celebrate others' failures?

Do they blame everyone but themselves?

Do they expose secrets that aren't theirs?

This reveals their character.

Trust what their behavior says—not what their mouth says.

Not everyone wants you to win.

Some people pretend to support you but quietly hope you fail.

They fear your growth because it challenges their comfort, threatens their ego, exposes their stagnation, highlights their insecurities.

You will see it in subtle comments, downplaying your achievements, fake concern, silent jealousy, sudden distance when you succeed.

This is normal.

Not everyone is meant to celebrate you.

Real supporters feel like sunlight—they don't dim when you rise.

Learn to observe without absorbing.

You don't need to internalize every emotion or intention around you.

You can observe someone's behavior without reacting, absorbing, personalizing, or overthinking.

Observation gives you wisdom.

Absorption drains your peace.

Be aware, not affected.

Set boundaries without guilt.

You do not need permission to protect your mental health, emotional stability, peace, goals, energy.

If someone respects you, they respect your boundaries.

If they don't, they were benefiting from your lack of boundaries.

Boundaries expose intentions.

Separate people by category.

Not everyone deserves the same level of access.

There are people you enjoy, people you learn from, people you help, people you work with, people you love from a distance, people you must avoid completely.

Clarity prevents confusion.

Categorize people correctly.

The way someone treats you is a reflection of their inner world.

If someone mistreats you, it's not because you are unworthy—it's because they are unhealed.

If someone respects you, it's because they respect themselves.

If someone lies to you, it's because they lie to themselves.

If someone supports you, it's because they are secure enough to uplift others.

People project their inner world outward.

When you understand this, you stop asking,

"Why are they like this?"

And start saying,

"This is who they are. Let me act accordingly."

Understanding people frees you.
Understanding people protects you.
Understanding people gives you peace.

CHAPTER 18—LOVE WITHOUT LOSING YOURSELF

Love is powerful, beautiful, and transformative—but many people enter love without understanding how to protect themselves inside it.

Real love elevates your life.

Unhealthy love drains it.

The most important truth is this:

Love is not supposed to cost you your identity.

Love is supposed to strengthen it.

Love should add to your life, not replace it.

When love is healthy, you still have goals, you still have boundaries, you still have habits, you still have independence, you still have identity, you still have self-respect.

Losing yourself for someone is not love—it's self-abandonment.

You should never have to disappear just to be valued.

Do not pour into someone who refuses to pour into themselves. You cannot save someone from their trauma, their insecurity, their laziness, their irresponsibility, their lack of self-respect, or their emotional chaos.

Love cannot replace self-work.

A relationship is not where someone goes to hide from their problems.

It is where two people go to grow together.

Do not let someone turn you into a bandage for their wounds.

Love requires boundaries, not blur.

Boundaries protect your mental health, your time, your energy, your peace, and your purpose.

A healthy partner respects your boundaries.

They do not guilt you, punish you, or pressure you for having them.

Where there are no boundaries, there is no balance.

Where there is no balance, love becomes draining.

Pay attention to how someone loves themselves.

A person's relationship with themselves sets the tone for how they will love you.

If they avoid responsibility, neglect their growth, speak negatively about themselves, tolerate disrespect, chase validation, lie to themselves, or settle for chaos, they will bring those same patterns into the relationship.

You cannot expect someone to love you better than they love themselves.

Real love requires truth, not perfection.

A healthy relationship needs honesty, communication, accountability, humility, and transparency.

Perfect people do not build strong relationships.

Truthful people do.

You do not need to be flawless.

You need to be willing to grow.

Love is not possession—it is partnership.

If someone tries to control you, isolate you, limit you, manipulate you, or suppress you, that is not love.

Love expands you.

Love supports your growth.

Love celebrates your evolution.

Love encourages your independence.

Love is two whole people choosing each other—not two broken people trying to complete each other.

Do not ignore the early signs.

Red flags do not disappear with time.

They intensify.

Patterns, tone, inconsistency, emotional immaturity, avoidance, blame, disrespect, broken boundaries—these things do not fix themselves.

Love does not blind you.

Denial does.

When someone shows you who they are, pay attention the first time.

Love requires emotional maturity, not intensity.

Intensity feels exciting, but it is not stability.

Emotional maturity looks like calm communication, taking accountability, apologizing sincerely, controlling reactions, respecting boundaries, solving problems together, growing individually and together.

Maturity sustains love.

Intensity burns it out.

Love should feel peaceful more often than it feels dramatic.

Real love brings stability, security, safety, joy, calmness, and understanding.

If love constantly feels chaotic, confusing, draining, unpredictable, or overwhelming, it is not love—it is emotional turbulence.

Love doesn't feel like tension.

It feels like home.

The strongest love begins with self-love.

The way you treat yourself teaches others how to treat you.

When you respect yourself, honor your standards, protect your peace, invest in your growth, maintain your identity, and speak your truth, you attract people who can love you at that same level.

Self-love is not selfish.

Self-love is preparation.

You must know your worth before someone else can respect it.

Healthy love doesn't require losing yourself.

Healthy love requires bringing your full self.

CHAPTER 19—CHOOSING YOUR PATH

Life will offer you many paths—
the safe path,
the easy path,
the familiar path,
the pressured path,
and the path everyone else expects you to take.

But only one path belongs to you.

Choosing your path is not about picking what looks best on the outside.

It's about honoring the truth inside you.

It's about listening to the quiet voice within that knows where you belong and who you are meant to become.

Choosing your path is one of the most important decisions you will ever make.

The right path is often the hardest one to take.

The wrong path is easy because it requires nothing from you—no discipline, no courage, no growth.

The right path forces you to develop character, build resilience, face your fears, walk alone sometimes, make tough decisions, leave behind comfort, and evolve.

Greatness is forged in discomfort.

Purpose is found in challenge.

Your path will test you before it rewards you.

Your path won't make sense to everyone—and it shouldn't.

People who don't understand your calling will try to pull you into theirs.

They will question your choices.

They will doubt your direction.

They will minimize your dreams.

They will pressure you to stay where they are.

Do not let someone else's fear decide your life.

Your vision was not given to them.

It was given to you.

Your path is revealed through movement, not overthinking.

Many people get stuck because they wait for a sign, a guarantee, or the perfect moment.

But life rewards action, not hesitation.

Clarity comes from trying, failing, adjusting, learning, exploring, moving.

You cannot steer a parked car.

Take the first step.

The next step will appear.

Your path requires letting go of what no longer fits.

Every level of life requires a different version of you.

You must release old environments, old expectations, old identities, old dreams, old relationships, old habits.

You cannot enter a new chapter while carrying the weight of previous ones.

Letting go is not losing.

Letting go is upgrading.

Your path is shaped by discipline, not desire.

Desire can make you dream.

Discipline makes you unstoppable.

Your path requires consistency, focus, commitment, sacrifice, self-control, and responsibility.

You cannot walk a powerful path with weak habits.

Your habits are the bricks that build your future.

Your path becomes clear when you stop living for approval.

Approval is a prison.

If you live for people's opinions, you will die in their expectations.

To choose your true path, you must be willing to disappoint some people, walk alone, break social norms, defy expectations, trust yourself, and stand firm.

Approval gives you comfort.

Purpose gives you direction.

Choose purpose.

Your path expands every time you choose courage.

Courage opens doors that fear keeps closed.

Every time you take a risk, set a boundary, speak your truth, commit to growth, leave comfort, or pursue purpose, your path widens.

Courage is the compass that keeps you aligned with your destiny.

Your path is not meant to be compared.

Comparison blinds you to your own journey.

Someone else's chapter ten is not the same as your chapter three.

Someone else's advantage is not your disadvantage.

Someone else's success is not your failure.

You are not behind.

You are not late.

You are not lost.

You are becoming.

Move at your pace.

Honor your timing.

Respect your journey.

Your path will challenge you before it blesses you.

Every time you level up, resistance appears, doubt increases, obstacles show up, old patterns resurface.

This is not punishment.

This is initiation.

Life tests you to see if you are ready for what you asked for.

You must prove your commitment through persistence.

Your path is built with intention.

Your life changes when you start choosing your actions instead of drifting through them.

Live with intention.

Choose your thoughts.

Choose your habits.

Choose your boundaries.

Choose your friends.

Choose your environment.

Choose your standards.

Choose your direction.

Intention creates meaning.

Meaning creates fulfillment.

Fulfillment creates purpose.

The moment you choose your own path, you stop living accidentally and start living deliberately.

This is how you build a life that belongs to you.

CHAPTER 20—BUILDING A LIFE THAT OUTLIVES YOU

A meaningful life isn't measured by how long you live, but by what remains long after you're gone.

Most people spend their lives chasing money,

status,

recognition,

comfort,

distractions,

and temporary pleasure.

But none of these things will outlive you.

What lasts are the choices you make,

the people you impact,

and the truth you leave behind.

To build a life that extends beyond your time on this earth, you must live intentionally, purposefully, and with a vision bigger than yourself.

These are the principles that create legacy.

Live by values, not by trends.

Trends fade.

Values endure.

Your values shape your character, your relationships, your discipline, your reputation, and your influence.

A person with strong values becomes a reference point—someone others look to for stability and truth.

Values outlive noise.

Teach through your actions, not just your words.

People follow what you do more than what you say.

Your behavior becomes inspiration, guidance, standard, blueprint.

Integrity creates invisible impact.

The way you carry yourself teaches others how to live.

Many people you will never meet may shape their lives because of something you demonstrated quietly.

Build something bigger than yourself.

Legacy comes from creation.

Build a business, a body of work, a family, a mission, a message, a craft, a movement, a skill set, a mindset.

Creation is contribution.

What you build continues working long after you stop.

Invest in people, not just achievements.

Your impact is measured by the lives you influence.

Sometimes the smallest conversation, the smallest act of kindness, or the smallest piece of guidance changes someone's entire direction.

People never forget how you make them feel.

People never forget how you lifted them.

Human impact is the highest form of legacy.

Become someone others can rely on.

Be a person of stability, honesty, strength, discipline, truth, compassion, wisdom.

A reliable person becomes a foundation in the lives of others.

Your presence becomes a source of security and clarity.

Reliability builds legacy because it builds trust.

Leave the world better than you found it.

This doesn't require fame or wealth.

It only requires intention.

You leave the world better through acts of kindness, wisdom you share, people you help, cycles you break, love you give, truth you stand on, and standards you elevate.

Small contributions become large impact over time.

Break generational patterns.

You don't need to repeat what previous generations did.

You can break cycles of fear, silence, trauma, poverty, limitation, emotional suppression, self-neglect.

When you heal yourself, you heal those who come after you.

Breaking a pattern is a form of legacy.

Protect your name with your behavior.

Your name is a seed.

Everything you do plants something in it.

People will remember your character, your integrity, your standards, your discipline, your resilience.

Your name becomes your legacy.

Leave a name that means something powerful.

Live with purpose every day.

Legacy is not created in one moment—it's created in thousands of small moments.

It's built through consistent discipline, intentional decisions, thoughtful actions, quiet sacrifices, daily growth.

Legacy is the accumulation of your life's direction.

Become someone worth remembering.

This does not mean being perfect—it means being real, strong, and committed to your evolution.

People are remembered for their truth, their love, their wisdom, their strength, their courage, their authenticity, their impact.

Legacy is not what you leave behind.

It's who you become while you're here.

A life that outlives you is built through daily choices, deep integrity, and intentional truth.

Build with purpose.

Live with meaning.

Leave something that echoes.

CHAPTER 21—YOUR LIFE IS YOUR CREATION

Y our life is not an accident.
Your life is not a random series of events.
Your life is not something that simply "happens" to you.

Your life is your creation.

Every decision, every habit, every boundary, every truth, every moment of courage, every moment of discipline—
they all shape the direction your life takes.

You are not here to drift.
You are not here to follow the crowd.
You are not here to live according to other people's fears or expectations.

You are here to build.
You are here to rise.
You are here to become something powerful, grounded, wise, and fully alive.

The world will try to distract you.

People will try to influence you.

Fear will try to weaken you.

Comfort will try to trap you.

Old patterns will try to pull you back.

But remember:

Nothing is stronger than a person who chooses themselves.

Choose your growth.

Choose your discipline.

Choose your truth.

Choose your future.

Choose your peace.

Choose your purpose.

You do not become great by accident.

You become great by intention.

The world will not hand you clarity—you must create clarity.

The world will not give you courage—you must practice courage.

The world will not give you freedom—you must build freedom.

The world will not give you purpose—you must live with purpose.

Everything you need is already inside you:

The strength.

The wisdom.

The intuition.

The resilience.

The greatness.

The discipline.

The ability to evolve.

Life is not about becoming someone else.

It is about uncovering the strongest version of who you already are.

So take the next step.

Trust yourself.

Honor your path.

Protect your peace.

Grow with intention.

Walk with purpose.

Stand in your truth.

The world changes when one person decides to live awake.

Let that person be you.

Your life is your message.

Write it with intention.

Live it with courage.

Leave it with meaning.

This is your journey.

This is your responsibility.

This is your creation.

Go build the life that only you can build.

EPILOGUE—WHEN YOU ARE READY TO BEGIN

You have reached the end of this book, but not the end of your journey.

Everything you read is now a part of you:

The clarity.

The wisdom.

The strength.

The awareness.

The discipline.

The truth.

The world will still challenge you.

People will still test your peace.

Life will still demand your courage.

But now you walk differently.

You walk awake.

You walk aware.

You walk with intention.

You walk with purpose.

You walk carrying the truths that most people never discover.

This is not the end.

This is the moment your real path begins.

Go forward with strength.

Go forward with peace.

Go forward with purpose.

The world will try to distract you.

Stay aligned.

The path will get difficult.

Stay disciplined.

People will misunderstand you.

Stay grounded.

You already have what you need.

You already know what matters.

You already carry the truth.

Now—

go live it.

AFTERWORD

Before you close this book,
I want to leave you with something deeper than advice
and stronger than motivation.
A blessing for your mind, your path, and your life.

May you always protect your peace,
even when the world tries to shake it.

May you always honor your truth,
even when others cannot understand it.

May you always choose courage,
even when fear feels louder.

May you always walk with clarity,
even when life becomes complicated.

May you always guard your energy,
even when people pull at your strength.

May you always rise above your old patterns,
even when comfort tries to pull you back.

May you always remember who you are,
especially in moments when the world tries to make you forget.

May you build a life that reflects your highest self,

not your lowest doubts.

May you give love without losing yourself,

and receive love without shrinking who you are.

May you see the truth early,

learn quickly,

grow boldly,

and live consciously.

May your heart stay steady,

your mind stay sharp,

your spirit stay grounded,

and your purpose stay alive.

And above all—

May you walk through this world awake,

unshakeable,

at peace,

and fully alive.

You are stronger than you know.

You are wiser than you realize.

You are more capable than you've ever been told.

Carry these truths with you.

Return to them when you need them.

Live them with intention.

This is your blessing.

This is your reminder.

This is your light.

Go forward with strength.

Go forward with clarity.

Go forward with purpose.

Your life is yours.
Now go create it.

ABOUT THE AUTHOR

Ralph Clotaire Jean is a thinker, writer, and observer of the human experience whose work focuses on clarity, strength, awareness, and purpose.

Through years of reflection, inner discipline, and deep study of human behavior, he developed a simple yet powerful philosophy:

Life becomes easier when you learn to see it clearly.

Growing up without guidance, Ralph learned early that the world rarely teaches people how to navigate life with truth.

Every lesson he gained came through firsthand experience—through watching people, learning from patterns, overcoming challenges, and asking the questions most people avoid.

Instead of letting confusion shape him, he turned understanding into his mission.

Driven by the desire to give his children—and anyone willing to grow—the wisdom he had to learn the hard way, Ralph wrote *My Voice* as a guide to navigating the world with strength, discipline, self-awareness, and unshakable purpose.

His writing is known for being:

Simple yet profound.

Direct yet compassionate.

Practical yet timeless.

Gentle yet powerful.

Ralph believes that when a person learns how to understand themselves, protect their peace, and see the world clearly, they become unstoppable.

My Voice is his first major written work, created as both a legacy for his children and a universal manual for anyone seeking truth, direction, and personal mastery.

9 798994 880623